THE HIDDEN DIVINE KEY

TO

EVERYTHING

BY

Angelo O. Oneka

TABLE OF CONTENTS

Introduction

This modern world has all kinds of problems. Some of these problems can easily be handled while others are not easy to handle. They are so complex and mind consuming that may require either a professional or some powers to handle. This being the case, many people, normally find themselves fully surrounded with no hope of escape. They may try different things to overcome the problems yet without any success.

This book is written purposely to help you overcome these intricate problems. It will expose you to some heavenly powers that will eradicate your persistent problems permanently and thus give you room for peace of mind, good health and progress.

If you put to use what you will read in this book, you should see your problems totally eradicated. You will also be able to witness complete developmental progress in your life.

CHAPTER ONE

WEALTH

Wealth is something that everyone desires. Everyone wants to have easy life. The life that one does not have to struggle or have to run around looking for money to solve one's problems or to put food on the table.

In all the years I have lived, I have never heard anyone say or wish to be poor. Although, I for one made that crazy mistake one time when I wish I was poor, and indeed my wish came true, and I paid for it so dearly. Like they say, " Do not wish for something or you may get it". I got it. However, herein I am appealing to you to always wish for something good in your life. It is never a wrong thing to wish for wealth because God Almighty Himself is the provider of wealth. It is totally wrong to say that God does not want us to be rich under the pretext of materialism. God is the one that blesses us to become rich. It was God who made King Solomon rich. It was God that blessed Abraham. It was God that blessed famous King David to be rich. It is God who has blessed Bill Gates with billions of dollars, and the list goes on and on endlessly. Tomorrow if God wants you to become a billionaire, will you say no because it is materialism? I do not think so, you will just say yes God and thank you very much. You know for sure your life will change drastically.

God wants us to be comfortable. He wants us to have everything so that we do not have to worry about anything and turn away from Him in pursuit of these things that we require in life. Example of God wanting us to have everything is in the creation itself. God created practically everything we require or need in life. He created fruits, he created animals for meat for us, fish, birds, vegetables, water, air, on and on, and gave us free of charge. Do not tell me that they are not free! Yes they are free, but the greedy human beings decided to commercialize them. You will argue that you worked for them. Didn't God work for them? In that aspect, let me pose two questions to you. When did you ever pay for these things to God? And how much did you pay for them? If you can answer these questions affirmatively, that then makes me wrong and a liar, if not, then the truth prevails and that truth will set me free.

Looking for wealth

Are you in search of wealth? Where do you go to look for it? My friend, I have an answer for you. Wealth is everywhere you do not have to look for it. First seek God and He will provide you with the wealth that you are desperately looking for. Your own efforts alone will never ever make you become wealthy. You need the blessings of God Almighty in order to become wealthy. If you rely on your own efforts alone, then you are walking on a quick sand and you will never reach your destination of wealth creation. Nor will your intellect or wisdom make you rich. How many very intelligent people of the world, are swimming in abject poverty? Countless my friend. It is God Almighty who will make you wealthy. When you have God, then you have everything and that is undisputable fact. Who created gold, the source of our money? It is God Almighty. And is it too difficult for God to make you become rich overnight? No, it is completely nothing to God. God can instantly turn you into a millionaire from a bum. Therefore put your trust in God from whom all good things come, and He will give you your heart's desire. You do not need to look any further but just work hard to find God for your blessings and solutions.

Prayer

In your pursuit of wealth, pray to God. And when you pray to God Almighty, you do not just say random prayer. Be specific, for example, if you have come to God for wealth, therefore, ask for wealth. You can't hide your intention from God. He already knows your intention, and if you just hide your intention, He will just laugh at your hypocrisy and thus deny you what you actually came for but then give you the hypocritical request. If you go to a doctor for treatment of a headache, do you tell the doctor that you have the stomach upset? What treatment will the doctor give you then? Of course he or she will prescribe for you the medicine for stomach. And then when you are out of his or her clinic, you will call him or her a fool. A fool for your own mistake and hypocrisy! God at times, work like that to drive senses in our head and at the same time seems to tell us, next time, don't be a hypocrite. Therefore if you go to God for wealth do not beat about the bush, just tell Him, you came for wealth and let Him give you the reason for denial. God's denial reasons normally surface if only we can pay close attention.

Many people including those preachers when they go to God, they wonder around in their prayers and thus leave without solutions from God because they were hypocritical in their prayers. If you go to God always be specific, God is a very good listener, He will never get you wrong, tell Him head on and waste no time. Instead of one hundred words, you may need only ten words. Know that God has so many people in line waiting to talk to him, the briefer you are, the understood you are and thus the provision of appropriate solutions. God is not going to spend the whole day with you when He has a lot to attend to, including the tiny things like the insects. Do not think that it is only us that pray to God, even trees and grass pray to God for rain and sunshine. This is the spiritual realm aspect. If you can tell God your request even in two words, the better, but be specific for the correct solutions.

Fasting

Fasting is supposed to be even more specific. People fast for specific problems. That is the way. If you are fasting for healing, for example, you do not declare your fast to God as a fast for wealth. It is a total contradiction. Therefore, instead of healing that you went for, you may end up with wealth instead. It does not work that way, I can assure you. Always be very specific in your fast in order to get the result you require.

Always make the intention known

Before you begin your fast, make your intention known to God, that is, what you are going to fast for. It is again the same principle like in prayers. You specifically fast for what you want. It does not make sense when your intention is wealth and you contradictorily fast for health. This kind of fast defeats the logic and you may not get an answer to that fast. However, you can fast for several things at once provided you lay them to God before you begin your fast, but remember to stick only to the list.

At the end of the day when you are completing your fast and before you put anything in your mouth, go on your knees and tell God that you have come to the end of your day fast, again list remind Him of what you are fasting for. I mean list those demands that you are fasting for. Again, be very specific, just hit the nail on the head instead of rumbling. Once again, God has no time to waste. He has the whole universe to attend to. From germs to the whales. So be concise in tendering your request to Him.

Worship

Worship is a gate-key to open the gate of heaven. When you worship, you are literally opening the gate of heaven in order for you to enter the Kingdom of God.

When you are going to pray for anything, always try your very best to start with worship and let the door be open for you to go before God Almighty.

Worship is pleasing to God Almighty. It is like songs of praises to the earthly leaders. When these earthly leaders hear the songs that praise them, they become so happy and so is it with God Almighty. God loves praises and all He requires from us, are the praises. What else can you give to God that He does not have? God needs nothing else from us, for all these things are His. Do you think you can please me when you take what is mine and give me as a gift? Not even an insane person will be pleased, if anything, he or she may attack you for that. But when you praise and exalt me, then I see the real follower and someone with love, and at the moment, when you ask me for anything I can afford to give, you will have it.

Always try your best to praise God Almighty that you may come closer to Him. God wants human friends by the way, that is why He was coming and talking to some people in the past, remember Abraham, Jacob, etc. And God Almighty has not changed a bit. He can still be your friend and talk to you. Some people may say that is not possible. Yeah it is not possible from your own angle but with God Almighty, it is more than possible.

Things you should do and not do

1. Start your request with a worship
2. Be specific in your prayer
3. Avoid being too wordy and do not rumble
4. Do not have ill-intention or your prayer or fast won't be answered
5. Forgive that you may be forgiven and your request granted
6. When you fast, fast for specific reason
7. When you pray, do not let your mind wonder from one thing to another. Close your mind to everything else except what you are praying for.
8. Believe that your prayer has been answered
9. You can also start your prayer with thanks giving
10. When you pray, choose a quiet place
11. When you pray, talk to God like you are talking to your friend, remember prayer is talking and presenting our petitions to God Almighty.
12. Do not steal. If you steal, it will block the blessing that was prepared for you.
13. Do not cheat. Again cheating may block any of the blessings that was meant for you. Let us say that God had prepared for you a blessing of one million dollars, but before that blessing came, you cheated someone of ten dollars. For that, you may forfeit one million dollars for ten dollars, you got wrongfully. Is it worth it? Absolutely not, so therefore be honest that you may receive your blessings.

CHAPTER TWO

HEALTH

Are you in poor health? If so, it is not by accident that you are reading this book. This book will provide you with essential information to a road to recovery. It is the divine healing that you are going to get from this book. And divine healing is more important than getting cured. Because in curing or treatment, sometimes the disease or sickness may recur, but divine healing will permanently put to rest your disease, sickness or pain.

Let me ask you a question, a mechanic, and a manufacturer of a vehicle who is also involved in the repair of vehicles, who has a better clue to repair the vehicles from this same manufacturer? The answer to this question is a no brainer, it is a manufacturer who has a better clue. For the manufacturer has full knowledge of how these vehicles function. Besides, the manufacturer has the original spares for these vehicles.

Here in this case, God Almighty is the manufacturer (creator) and a doctor is like a mechanic. He or she only repairs but has no thorough knowledge about human body as compared to God's knowledge. Sometimes like a mechanic that may mess up your vehicle, a doctor may also mess up your health but God will not. That is a divine healing. Have you never heard or seen, some people admitted in the hospitals with specific sickness but they come out with more health problems, with God this can never happen and that is a divine healing. In so saying, I am not advocating for you not to go to the hospitals, because hospitals are surely important, but I am making a true comparison between treatments and divine healing.

God the Creator

God created all of us. He is a great designer. He skillfully designed us, our organs, limbs, etc. He knows what they came from, and what ingredients were used to make them. Our bodies are not a result of evolution but a result of creation. God also knows how our bodies function. Everything in our bodies were scientifically designed to precision. And all the parts of our bodies are programed to work in unity. That is not by accident but by advanced knowledge of science and technology.

When it comes to divine healing, God has in place all the spare organs that He can use to replace the worn out ones. And this can be done with great precision and without any side effects whatsoever. The thorough knowledge He has, does not require Him to read the labels of the organs in the process of replacements. This tells you that divine healing is without faults. And once you receive it, you should worry less of the aftermath.

In case of sickness/illness

In case of sickness, when everything here on earth has failed, don't be alarmed. You have been from one doctor to another but without any cure. Let me tell you specifically not to be alarmed. It is not yet over. You will still have your health and future. There is a God the creator. He is a miracle Himself.

Now that all the treatments you have received have failed you, it is time now for you to go to God Almighty the greatest physician, where the word failure is unheard of. Where cancer drops and melts like the wax. Where the word incurable does not exist. Where miracles are the order of the day. For with God, everything is possible.

You are not going to spend years in the hospital receiving treatments to get cured, but you will get instant healing. And when you are healed, everything replaced in your body is new. They are like at the time you came to this world. They will not bother you and there are no complications or side effects, they are just perfect. That is the miracle of divine healing as opposed to treatments.

What to do and to know to get divine healing

1. The first and the most important thing, is to believe in the existence of God Almighty. God does exist. He is real more than one hundred percent. This is a reality and undisputable truth. Whether you believe in His existence or not, does not in any way alter the fact of His existence.

If anything, the disbelief merely and narrowly defines you to stupidity. One day, He will reveal Himself to you, let me hope is not going to be a very painful revelation. However, let me concretely assure you that God Almighty exists.

2. He is omnipotent
3. He is omniscient
4. He is omnipresent
5. He is authoritative, however, not meaning that He is a dictator. God is generous and liberal, that is why He freely gave us total freedom to do anything. And total freedom of choice. You choose what to do and God never interferes. He has powers to do anything and yet, He is kind.
6. He is protective. God protects us twenty four seven and three hundred and sixty five days.
7. He is generous. Look around, the fruits you have on the table, which factory manufactured them? The water you drink and to make drinks that you drink, who created it? Or was it a factory in the world that manufactured it? The air that you breathe to keep alive, who created it or which factory in the world manufactured it? And what is the name of that factory? Practically, everything we need in life, God Almighty created them, but the greedy human beings now exploit his fellow human beings by selling them. In the case of air, God Almighty saw the greed of human beings well in advance, and said to Himself, I am not going to give them dominion of this, lest they deprive their fellow human beings to death. And air has remain under the control of God Almighty.
8. Pray for your healing unceasingly until you receive it. Do not ever give up. Continue to pray even if you feel lazy to pray or even when you are deceived that you are not receiving it. Pray when in pain and when not in pain. You can pray quietly on your sick bed, you do not necessarily have to kneel down. God looks at our hearts, He knows whether you are sincere or not, position to Him means nothing but it is our hearts that is a true revelation of sincerity and love. Again like I said earlier, always be specific. You need your damaged heart replace, tell Him you need a new heart to replace the damaged one. And He will make a replacement that is not short lived and without complications whatsoever. If you need a kidney, tell God you need a kidney. And if you need new lungs, tell God you need new lungs, etc. We do not receive because we do not ask or we are misled to believe that it is never feasible.

   However, Should God Almighty provide you with any of these new organs, do not ever go back to what destroyed the previous ones, for that would mean an insult to God Almighty. And when you receive healing, that means God has given you a new part but when you are cured, it means that part is merely repaired.

9. If it is not against doctors' directives, fast for your healing if you can. Again, let God Almighty know your intention before you begin the fast. Tell Him, God Almighty, I am fasting for the healing of---then name that part that you want to be healed. And if healing does not come after the fasting period, do not be in despair and doubts, but continue to believe that your new organ is on the way coming. I guarantee you, it will come but may come when you least expect it. You do not know when and you do not know how, but God Almighty knows it.

Are you now a terminal patient

Are you now terribly hill? Have they told you that you have only few days to live? No, it is not going to happen, thank God that you have this book in your hand, for you are going to live, I mean to live. And if it is you the relatives having this book in your hands, believe it, he or she is going to live. Right now and without wasting time, take your case or his or her case to God Almighty the giver of life, close your eyes and forget everything else but enter in the presence of God Almighty with the request for life. Petition God earnestly for your life, his life or her life. Also believe firmly now in the restoration of life and the healing from God Almighty. Listen, with God everything is possible.

Pray even if you are only able to utter only one word, and that one word must be that organ that is trying to kill you. Firmly believe in your heart that you have been healed by God Almighty and receive your healing. Let me tell you, you are going to live, God Almighty is going to heal you. That sickness will flee because of God Almighty. And you will receive a new organ from God that is free from any attack of any disease, because, it is a special gift from God Almighty. God put this book in your hand for that purpose. You are going to live and nothing will stop that. GOD is power. Life is yours and death is vanquished.

CHAPTER THREE

HUSBAND

Every good husband is a gift from God Almighty. If God has not given you a good husband, you will always have problems in the family. Peace will be totally absent in the family, and peace of mind, will always elude you. Your marriage instead of being a paradise will turn out to be hell on earth.

If you have a bad husband

If you have a bad husband, the one that will always give you different kinds of problems, such as infidelity, quarrelling, fighting, etc, do not confront him with a similar behaviour or attitude, rather be reconciliatory and forgiving. In your step to fight this injustice and win him over, turn to God who created him and let Him deal with him.

Present your case to God Almighty precisely and on a daily basis. Do not ever give up, saying you are tired of praying, but continue the fight relentlessly. The time you are about to give up, may be also the time God wants to answer your prayer, so continue praying until you get an answer to your prayer. Nor should you think of abandoning the marriage, for that may make the matter even worse for you. When you leave, you will begin to feel sorry for having left, and at the same time, you will miss him terribly because you were already used to one another, and this may send you into depression. Remember, you can never win by quitting, hang on until the day breaks. If you think of remarrying, you may pull yourself from the oven right into the fire. You may get married to the worst man ever. Also by the mere fact that he might be confusing you and committing adultery with you, in itself tells you precisely what type of man he is. Do you trust such kind of person? If you do, you do so at your own peril. You will dance to the tune of cheating and disloyalty. Are you going to quit again? If you do, that will surely be your pattern in life and that also will automatically group you in the group of harlots from other people's point of view.

If you keep on hopping around, people will not like you, it gives you terrible reputation and you may have few friends. Other men would not want you to associate with their wives because they think you will spoil them too. Remember, any problem can be solved however intricate it may be, all one needs is to apply sophisticated solution to such intricate problem. You can win the fight from within rather than turning your back to the fight and become quite an easy target. Just be patient, stay on but strategize your fight to win him over. During this period, devote your time to fully study him, know his strengths and weaknesses and apply the sophisticated formula to solve this persistent problem. There are many ways you can fully overcome this guy. One of your strategies, should be bed affairs, it is your absolute God's given right. I am being open and calling a spade, a spade and not a big spoon. Is not everybody aware of that? And the most powerful weapon is of course God Himself. Pray and leave everything to God and God who sees your daily sufferings will take appropriate action. Who is this man to God? When God is done with him, you will not ever recognize him anymore, it is like God has thrown from heaven an angel to become your husband. He will be sweeter than honey.

Show and sow love

Love is a very powerful weapon that one can use to overcome an enemy or a problem. Love intoxicates and drives one to submission consciously or unconsciously.

When your situation becomes so critical with constant numerous problems, such as fights, quarrels, and so on, show love. At this peril time, you should show more love than you have ever shown before. Let it drive senses into his head. One day his eyes will be wide open to a complete reality and shame. His injustice will manifest within, accompanied by conviction of truth. His eyes and the heart will be opened to the injustice he has been perpetrating on you. Fight on never give up.

When your war is over and the change takes place, you will have the total peace that you had been yearning for. Love is a very powerful weapon to overcome any situation. If he insults you, tell him, I love you. If he ignores you, tell him, I love you. Make him look a fool. Continue in this process until one day, he will say to himself, wait a minute, maybe I am stupid and crazy. Why is she always good to me even though I am bad to her? This will certainly be a turning point in your fight for justice. Remember, even the toughest iron can be reshaped. Who is he that he can't change? I can assure you, he can change for the better.

Fasting

If your prayer alone is not working, combine it with fasting. These are the two most powerful weapons to fight any situation in life. When everything else has failed, use the prayer and the fast to overcome him. As I said earlier, before you start to fast, make your intention known to God Almighty. Try this and see the result by yourself.

Do not involve other people in your domestic conflict

Even if the situation becomes so critical, never involve other people in your conflict, because they may simply make the matter worse. They may tell your spouse behind you all kinds of things, and you will be very sorry that you ever involved such kind of people in your domestic affairs. You can solve your problems much better than trying to use other people to solve them for you.

The day you involve other people in your conflict, is also they the day things will change for the worse. If you were still on talking terms, you will no longer be on talking terms. The conflict will rapidly escalate to your total amazement. As they draw closer to you, the nearest is also the destruction of your marriage. These may be the devils in the disguise of counsellors, leave them far away and save your marriage. You have brains, you are not kids, besides you know the very source of your problems, tackle the problems head on.

In solving your problems, leave no stone unturned. Exhaust every single issue right from the foundation. And totally destroy the foundation for the new beginning. Call a spade, a spade because you want to fully resolve the problems.

Create a parliament in your family where you can sit down and educationally and amicably discuss any issue that may be a thorn in the flesh for the family. Open discussions without hiding anything in your heart will surely lead you to the very foundation of the problem. When you find or reach that foundation, totally destroy it, and in its place, erect the pillar of peace and love. And also the guilty party should strictly promise no repeat of the mistake and the offended offers forgiveness. With these, you have the foundation built on a rock.

Never involve the children

For any problem between the two of you, never ever involve your children in or you will make the situation to explode. This is because children have divided love. Some may love the mother more, while others may love the father more. So if you involved them, the other party that is not loved will totally be victimized by the discussion, because it will be a one-sided support for the one that is loved. This may irate the unloved party and thus create hatred not only towards the spouse but also the children. It will also make the situation more volatile than before and that may set the stage for break-up, separation or divorce.

If you have a problem, simply discuss it just between the two of you. The best time to discuss such an issue should be at night when the children are asleep and after making love. The love affairs is a very powerful tool for appeasement and negotiations between the spouses. However, do not manipulate the issue and your spouse because of this, otherwise, you have not solved your problem. Love affair gives you total room for serious discussion without any involvement of anger because anger had been vanquished at that moment. Why? Because the love affairs always bring you closer to one another and is also taming. Make sure at this moment, the opportune moment, you exhaust all the issues at length and hammer a concrete agreement at that given time.

Do not ever involve your relatives

Your relatives can only make matters worse because they will always support you, even when you are wrong, and this may annoy your spouse, thus worsen the situation. Very few relatives may be quite open and tell you that you are wrong, otherwise most of them will ten to support you.

By supporting you blindly or intentionally, they are merely destroying your marriage. And if you allow this to happen and your marriage is destroyed, you will hate them for what they have done to you and your marriage although you were literally happy with them at the time of discussion. Therefore avoid this kind of involvement altogether.

CHAPTER FOUR

WIFE

The Bible makes it clear that to have a good wife is a gift from God Almighty. That is really true because not all the wives are good wives just like not all the husbands are good husbands. As there are terrible husbands, there are also terrible wives who can drive you really crazy on daily basis.

Does it therefore mean you should get rid of her? The answer is a complete no. The best you can do is to get to the core of the problem. May be she is sick mentally, you do not know. May be something is really disturbing her, you do not know, the list may go on and on endlessly. How about your behaviour? May be it is contributing to this, you do not know. That is why you should dig deeper into the problem before you ignorantly get rid of her.

If you are messing around, you could seriously be contributing to her unwanted behaviour. The question of infidelity is a very serious issue that grossly affects anybody regardless of gender or status and is always the core issue to divorce. Therefore check up your own behaviour first before you condemn and decide to get rid of her.

Seek audience with her

Do not sweep the rubbish under the carpet. Take heart, and sit down with her and discuss issues at length and amicably. Request her to be open and you too be open with her, because it does not pay to hide anything in your heart. If you decide to hide anything in your heart, you are not in anyway, going to solve the problem. Instead of uprooting the carrot, you are merely cutting the stems, and that therefore means the carrot will grow deeper and bigger. Your problems will also grow deeper and bigger if any of you decides to hide anything instead of bring it up on the table for pertinent discussion.

Be open, let out everything. That way, you are getting to the very core of the problem that is haunting and tearing you apart. Remember, you did not marry in order to have problems, be unhappy or be depressed, but you married to be happy and enjoy life. Who wants to be married to have hell on earth type of life? Not you, not me and sure enough, not anybody.

Also remember that if you do not discuss your problems, that automatically signifies that your marriage is on the brink of collapse, and surely it will stop to exist. Whose fault will it be? Of course, it will squarely be your own fault because you did not take the initiative to handle it. However, if you try and she is not co-operating, then the fault will be hers. And in case of break-up, she will regret it later on, which will then be too late. They say pride goes before a fall.

Fights and quarrels

Beware that you cannot always solve any problem by fighting or quarrelling. In the pursuit of this direction, you can only make the matters worse, unless your intention is to get rid of her. Why would you want to do that anyway? What if it were you, would you be happy? Know that what is bad for you is also bad for another person. How huge is the problem? Have you given it all the trials and never worked? Has she become a complete nuisance? Weigh all these in before your action. I know some people do not understand until they see the light, anyhow be fair and still give it a chance. Know that taking arbitrary actions is a prelude to more serious problems.

Always try your very best to solve the problem before you make a decision that can not only hurt the other party, but also you. Before any action, make sure that you thoroughly investigate into the problem.

Forgiveness

In your discussion, if you find any fault unless it is very serious, always try to forgive. May be whatever happened, was not intended. Be human in your approach in solving the problem. As the saying goes, 'to err is human', we all have our weaknesses. What you must know is that forgiveness at times opens the eyes of the guilty. Again I say forgive and let the person see his or her fault and with it, may come repentance and also total change of behaviour. Forgiveness may be the fire to bend the unbendable iron.

God Almighty

Everything in life hinges on God Almighty. He pulls the strings. No matter how intelligent, no matter how hardworking, no matter how much we try, for us to succeed, God Almighty must endorse what we are trying to achieve, or else, we are merely wasting our time and energy.

Even if something looks so simple, if God does not permit us to achieve it, all our efforts driven towards achievement, will just be in vain.

So if you have tried your best to solve any problem, but have not made any headway, then it is high time that you took the problem to God Almighty, and let Him handle the problem. Any persistence will only frustrate you, make you lose more hair of your head, depress you, age you, or even kill you.

Go to God in prayer and fast. And do not give up until you get an answer. If you are doing the right thing, surely God will answer. Sometimes it may come immediately, at times, you may have a delayed answer, but do not give up.

If however God decides not to answer, that means, He sees a bigger problem ahead and because He does not want you to be in that problem, He will not answer. It may hurt you and it may break your heart, but later on you will appreciate it.

CHAPTER FIVE

EMPLOYMENT

Employment is an engine of survival. With employment, one is able to support a family, to fulfil some of the promises and aspirations.

Employment provides one with the money that we desperately need in this modern time in order to survive. Survival without money these days is near impossible, because everything now requires money. Money now has totally enslaved us, and we have to work in order to get it. Without work, we shall be penniless and that may lead to so many other problems, sometimes including the disintegrations of families. It looks like these days, the strength of marriage is based on money.

God and employment

As I stated earlier, everything good comes from God Almighty and this includes the employment that one has. If God is pleased with you, He will provide you with very good employment. Remember, King David, King Solomon, King Saul, Samuel the prophet and ruler of Israel, etc, were placed in their positions by God Almighty. God can do the same for you today. All you need to do, is to love and trust God. Also know that He is the provider of the food you eat to keep you alive.

For all these good things to happen to you, you need to go to God in prayer and fast. These two things can bring you closer to God Almighty and they can also open the door for you.

We have already looked at how you should pray, and what to do, when you are going to fast. Be open with God Almighty and never mince your words, tell God the type of job you would like to have. Do not be general in your request for the job but be specific. Hit the nail right on the head. If you want to be a Prime Minister, tell God Almighty just that. If you want to be a court clerk, tell God Almighty just that. It is pointless for you to be general, or you may end up with the type of job you do not like, and then you may blame God for that. Remember, you just asked for a job and you got the job, you did not ask for a specific job. Whose fault is it? Is it God's fault? No, it is absolutely your own fault. Had you asked for specific job, you would have got it.

Many people do not have their request granted because they do not know how to ask. Learn how to ask from God Almighty, always be specific. Also instead of being verbose, condense your words. Do not waste time thinking that by saying a lot, your request will be granted. No, it does not work that way because by being so wordy, you may lose your point completely, hence have no result.

Believe that you got it

Belief is a very powerful weapon when it comes to success. You must have faith. By faith, God Almighty created the whole universe. He simply said the words and things came to be. This same type of faith can work for you if you strongly believe in it and do not doubt. The problem with us human beings, is that, we say that we have faith but in reality we do not have it. For example, we may ask for something and believe only for a moment, and when a day passes without any happening, straight away we begin to doubt, even to the extent of asking ourselves whether this kind of thing had ever worked before. In short we are too full of doubts. Remember the case of Peter when he began to walk on the water with The Lord Jesus, doubt immediately attacked him. He began to question in his very heart, has any human being ever walked on the water? His heart told him, I don't think so, you are either dreaming or merely deceiving yourself, and he believed his heart. And at that very moment, he began to sink and he cried for help to The Lord Jesus, who then saved him from sinking. And he asked him, 'why did you doubt?' That is exactly how we human beings are, full of doubts, and because of doubts, we daily kill our would-be successes.

And when you killed the success by your negative faith, it is gone and gone forever. Do you think if The Lord Jesus was not there, would Peter still be alive at that very moment of doubt? No, he would have drowned and gone forever, history. And when you kill your success, it also becomes a mere myth. That therefore also means you negative faith has worked and you have received what you believed in, the doubt and the impossibility.

Do not ever do that if you want to achieve something, always believe that you have received it, even when a day, two days or three days pass without anything happening. Just continue in your belief and you will receive. Even if nothing of that can had ever happened. Just believe to the extent of madness, and if anybody knows of what you are believing in, would classify you in the group of mad people. Always learn to shut off negative faith right from a distance. Give it no chance to invade your mind thus denying you what you may desperately be wanting, something to die for. Always learn to say no to negative faith from within and from without. Therefore, now believe that you have been offered the job you applied for, supplement this with prayer and fast. Suffer for few days without food and water and receive the big reward.

CHAPTER SIX

PROMOTIONS

Promotion is something we all yearn for. When one receives promotion, one becomes extremely happy. We also celebrate when we receive promotions because they mean a lot to us. It enhances our social status, it also pushes our income up, and above all, it brings complete joy to our families. When we receive promotions, we also receive increase in our salaries. The promotion may also enable us to acquire such things as houses, vehicles, other valuable domestic assets such as refrigerators, freezers, televisions, etc.

How easy is it to get promotion?

Getting a promotion may not be that easy. We may have the right qualifications and be hardworking, yet, promotions may elude us. People with less education, less competent and less hardworking may be promoted to our disappointments. Some of these promotions happen because of nepotism, tribalism, racism or corruptions. This kind of promotion is totally unhealthy because it breeds incompetence and failures. Above all, it breeds total discouragement to other employees.

With discouragement thus come poor performances, poor product qualities, losses and poor services. At times, it also generates poor public relations, because the employees are not happy. Since they are not happy, they normally transfer their unhappiness on to the customers. As the mistreatments of customers begin to take root, the company may also begin to witness losses.

For the good of any organization, such kind of promotions should totally be discouraged.

What to do when promotions always pass you by

As I said earlier, you may have the right qualifications, be hardworking, and also, very disciplined, yet when it comes to getting promoted, you are always not in the list.

And as this trend continues unfolding, you are thus not only discouraged, but you also begin to question as to what is wrong with yourself. You also begin to wonder why you are always skipped. As you wonder why and become fully discouraged and sometimes depressed, you will also begin to charter a possible course of actions to be taken in order to fight this type of injustice. Quitting may also become part of your list of actions.

Anyhow let me ask you some few pertinent questions. What have you thought of? What steps have you taken? Have you totally given up?

If you have no clue and have totally given up, let me tell you herein, do not give up. You thought you have come to the end of the road, no you have not come to the end of the road. Know that even the mountain can be removed and the valley filled and the direction of the water flow diverted. Anything is possible and there is no problem without a solution.

You still have the way. The way to defeat your boss who has been wrongfully denying you the promotions you rightfully deserved. God Almighty is the victorious way that will never ever fail. Have you seen the immediate word that comes after the word God? The word is almighty. Almighty, that means He is all powerful with all the capabilities to do anything and beyond human comprehension.

Take your case to God Almighty in prayer and fasting. Let Him deal with your unjust boss. God has many ways to deal with your boss and He sees his or her injustice. And God hates injustices. He has many options to deal with your boss. Among others, He can have him or her immediately transferred, dismissed, become disabled or at worst even die. It is up to Him to decide which step is more appropriate.

When any of these happens, God may bring someone who may then give the favour you so deserved after having been deprived many times. He or she may give you the promotions that had for a long time, eluded you. I am not being mean here but that is a reality of the mysterious life. Certain bad things normally happen to pave the ways for the deprived ones and these are through divine powers.

Prayer

Just as I stated above, that you should go to God Almighty in prayer, I want to repeat here that always pray to God Almighty for the promotions you need. Tell Him why you need the promotions and what you will do with them. And as you pray, you should also work in your heart, try to clean all the dirt from your heart. Think of no revenge, or sitting on some people who are due for promotions. If you do this, God Almighty may not answer your prayer anymore. Be there to help the deprived and the helpless. Remember, a prayer from a clean heart is always answered by God.

Fasting

If you have tried prayer and the results are not forthcoming, combine this with a fast. Combined prayer and a fast can work wonders and can remove mountains. Now that you have had been denied promotions on a number of occasions, I want you to get those promotions that eluded you, by combining the prayer and a fast. Also ask God Almighty for forgiveness, for whatever wrong, you might have done to others, in order to speed up your promotions.

However, when God Almighty gives you these promotions that you desperately need, do not later on turn your back to God, begin to practise bad things or do bad things, or practise the same style that was practised on you. If you do any of these, you will receive worst punishments later on. They may come when you least expect them and in different forms. Be very careful and always thank God for what He has done for you. Also don't forget to do what is always right.

CHAPTER SEVEN

CHILDREN

Who is the provider of children? Clearly and without any reasonable doubt, God Almighty is the provider of children. God is the creator of human beings. He did that in the beginning and continues to do so today. His words "Let there be" are still working up to today. They were spoken once, and will continue to create endlessly.

The creation will only stop when God Almighty will withdraw His words. If He decides to say let there not be, then, the creation will cease to be. It is up to God Almighty Himself to decide and not us the human beings or any other creatures. God makes His own decisions and they are not influenced by any external forces. Some people may say that is complete garbage, God is not going to do that. My question is, how sure are you? Have you become God to make that statement? Do you now decide for God? Do you read God's mind? Do you think for Him and influence His decisions? If you can answer yes to all these questions, then I can believe you, otherwise, the truth still stands that God can decide to do anything anytime. It is purely His prerogative. He takes no order or advice from anyone.

Back to our topic, and let me begin by asking you some questions. Are you in need of having children? Have you tried everything and nothing has worked so far? Then it is time for you to decide to take your case to God Almighty, the creator, in prayer and fasting. Go to Him with pure heart, and power before Him the prayers for children. Do not feel sorry for yourself or cry, for God Almighty will help you. And it is never late because nothing is late for God Almighty. Also know that with God anything is possible. What we human beings think is totally impossible, it is always possible with God Almighty. I am showing you the way that will make you have children even though you have been laughed at. Forget about the laughter, and now embark on a mission to surprise those who have laughed at you.

SARA

Sara of Abraham had already passed her bearing age when the angel of God came to her. She had already given up hope of having children, and may be was only now waiting for death since she was already old.

One day the angel of Lord who was visiting, told her that she was going to have a child, but Sara looked at it as the biggest joke of the day and she laughed at that message. There was no way she could believe the angel of God, now that she was already too old for giving birth but with God, everything is possible.

The words of the angel came true. Sara had a baby boy and they name him Isaac meaning laughter, because Sara laughed at the message of an angel when he said she was going to have a baby. There is also a school of thoughts that Sara's baby was named Isaac or laughter possibly because people use to laugh at her because she had no child. Are the people laughing at you? Have you already passed your bearing age? Do not worry, those who are laughing at you know will be disappointed when God will give you a child or children. What is impossible with God Almighty? Absolutely nothing.

Simply go to God Almighty and present Him with your problem, cry to Him days and nights, and surely He will have compassion with you and provide you a child or children. When He does so, honour Him and do not forget Him like other people do. It is an insult to Him.

Anna

Anna the mother of Prophet Samuel was without a child and she was terribly grieved. You know human beings, I am sure she was also being laughed at by other people. In her pains, Anna turned to God Almighty the creator about her disturbing problem. She was always in the church crying out to God. And God Almighty saw her misery and decided to give her a child. They name that child Samuel. And because God was good to her in answering her prayer, Anna decided to dedicate that child to God and left him in the service of God.

God was with that child. He made him to become a great man, a prophet. God also made Samuel a leader or a judge of Israel.

If God Almighty could answer the prayer of Anna, He can also answer your prayer. Do not lose hope, hope is very much alive. You will have a child or children for nothing is impossible with God Almighty.

If prayer is taking too long, combine this with a fast. God is watching and listening to you, He also feels your pains. When you are petitioning God Almighty, avoid sinning for this will only complicate your case as well as block your prayer from being heard and answered. And if you had greatly sinned before, openly repent, tell the giving God that you are sorry of your past and sins, sincerely repent, and He will answer your prayer. When He answers your prayer, do not later go back to your vomit, or something very dreadful will happen to you later on when you least expect. Be wise and continue in the path of wisdom. Know that sins are the enemy of God. They separate man from God and also block our blessings leave alone causing death. Not only spiritual death but also physical death. Be very careful.

Also pray for the blessings of your children

When God Almighty answers your prayer, do not stop there but also continue to pray for the blessings of your children. Ask Him to bless them and make them great too. Most of the great people we have in the world were always prayed by their parents. Therefore, don't neglect your children, pray for them always and you will witness the power of The Mighty One. Remember, God holds the key to everything. You do not only want to have children, but also should want to have great children. The blessings of your children are also your blessings.

Pray for the good health and protection of your children

Always pray to God Almighty for the good health and protection of your children. You need God's protection from many of the unexpected in this world. It is only God who can protect your children, so therefore submit their lives into His hands. Those who are protected by God Almighty need not fear anything whether they are asleep or awake, whether they walk through the fire or the valley of death, include your children among those.

CHAPTER EIGHT

ANGER

There are always two types of enemies that we confront, and are always battling us. There is what we call an internal enemy and there are external enemies.

Internal enemy is more sophisticated and more difficult to fight, for we do not know when and from where it will attack us. For the external enemies, we are always on the alert but never with the internal enemy.

This internal enemy is more destructive than the external enemies. The internal enemy is part of us that is why it is so difficult to fight it. And anger is that internal enemy.

Anger strikes us any time when we least expect, and it normally completely subdues us. It does not give us any warning as to when and where it is coming from. And when it strikes, it leaves us totally helpless, makes us drunk and stupid. It also enables us to do things that we normally do not do. Its onslaught on us is astronomically destructive that when it leaves, one can still feel the after effects, probably for hours or even for days.

On the other end, the external enemies are normally easy to deal with. We know who they are and what they are capable of doing. And because of being fully aware of them and their activities, we normally tend to take extra precaution in order to prevent or deter their possible attacks on us, but this is never the case with an internal enemy.

However, there are no problems without solutions. Though internal enemy is a much complex enemy, yet, there are some solutions to handle it or deter it from attacking us, but first let us look at what the damage this internal enemy is capable of inflicting on us. Some of the damage the internal enemy is capable of inflicting on us are listed below.

What anger is capable of doing to us

There are several destructive things anger is capable of doing to us. Some of these are:

1. Anger can cause you heart attack

2. Anger can cause you high blood pressure
3. Anger can cause you a headache
4. Continuous anger may cause you cancer
5. Anger can cause you to fight
6. Anger can cause you to injure somebody
7. Anger may cause you to kill someone without any malice aforethought
8. Anger may cause you to start a war if you are a leader
9. Anger may cause your death
10. Anger may send you to jail
11. Anger may cause you, your relationship
12. Anger may destroy your marriage
13. Anger may cause you, your job
14. Anger may destroy your family
15. Anger may cause you to be dismissed from school
16. Anger may cause you to lose money
17. Anger may cause you stroke

How to fight anger

1. Perceive in advance the consequences of anger and your steps
2. Elevate yourself beyond what is happening
3. Ignore what might be causing you anger
4. Consider yourself matured to act stupidly
5. Ignore the person who is causing you anger
6. Walk away from whatever or whoever is causing you anger
7. Take a walk
8. Listen to good music that you like
9. Take a hot shower
10. Go to fresh air
11. Talk to someone you love
12. Do not stick it to your head
13. Just laugh at it off
14. Take a nap if you can
15. Drink a glass of water
16. Think of something funny that happened

www.ingramcontent.com/pod-product-compliance
Lightning Source LLC
Chambersburg PA
CBHW070941290526
45795CB00003B/1106